PIANO / VOCAL / GUITAR

# recollection

# THE BEST of NICHOLE NORDEMAN

ISBN-13: 978-0-634-08276-4
ISBN-10: 0-634-08276-0

7777 W. BLUEMOUND RD. P.O. BOX 13819 MILWAUKEE, WI 53213

Visit Hal Leonard Online at
**www.halleonard.com**

4     HOLY

12    TO KNOW YOU

20    THIS MYSTERY

27    EVERY SEASON

33    SUNRISE

41    BRAVE

52    LEGACY

61    FINALLY FREE

66    IS IT ANY WONDER?

72    I AM

79    WHAT IF

88    FOOL FOR YOU

96    EVEN THEN

104   WHY?

114   REAL TO ME

121   WHO YOU ARE

129   RIVER GOD

# HOLY

Words and Music by NICHOLE NORDEMAN
and MARK HAMMOND

Da da da _____ da da da da _____ da ya ya ya, _____ You are _____ ho- -ly. _____

How man-y roads _____ did I trav-

# TO KNOW YOU

Words and Music by NICHOLE NORDEMAN
and MARK HAMMOND

**Moderately slow**

It's well __ past mid-night and I'm a-wake __ with ques-tions that won't wait __ for day-light, sep-a-rat-ing fact __ from my i-mag- -i-nar-y fic-tion on this shelf of my __ con-vic-tion. I

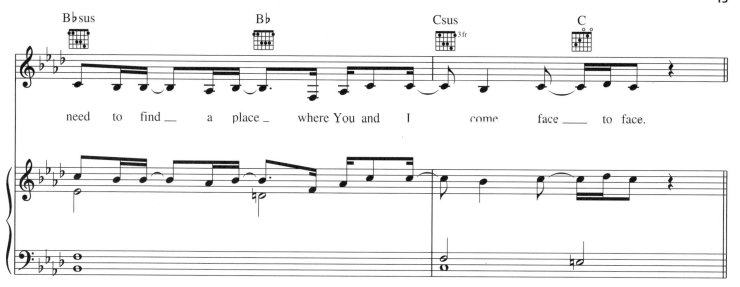

need to find ___ a place ___ where You and I come face ___ to face.

Thom - as need-ed proof that You ___ had real - ly ris - en
Nic - o - de-mus could not un - der - stand ___ how You could

un - de-feat - ed. When he placed ___ his fin - gers where the
tru - ly free ___ us. He strug-gled with ___ the im - age of a

nails once broke Your skin, _ did his faith fi-n'lly be-gin? ____ I've
grown man _ born a-gain. _ We might have been good friends, _ cuz

lied if I've _ de-nied _ the com-mon ground _ I've shared _ with him. ___ And I, _
some-times I ____ still ques-tion, too, how eas-i-ly we come to You. _ But I, _

_____ { I real-ly want _ to know _ You. I

18

# THIS MYSTERY

Words and Music by
NICHOLE NORDEMAN

# EVERY SEASON

Words and Music by
NICHOLE NORDEMAN

# SUNRISE

Words and Music by
NICHOLE NORDEMAN

# BRAVE

Words by NICHOLE NORDEMAN
Music by NICHOLE NORDEMAN and JAY JOYCE

# LEGACY

Words and Music by
NICHOLE NORDEMAN

I don't mind if you've got something nice to say about me, and I en-joy an ac-co-lade, like the rest, and you could take my pic-ture and hang it in a gal-ler-y of all the "who's

# FINALLY FREE

Words and Music by
NICHOLE NORDEMAN

# IS IT ANY WONDER?

Words and Music by
NICHOLE NORDEMAN

# I AM

Words and Music by
NICHOLE NORDEMAN

# WHAT IF

Words and Music by
NICHOLE NORDEMAN

D.S. al Coda

for ___ so _____ long. But what if you're _

___ wrong? _____

What if you _____ jump and just close ____

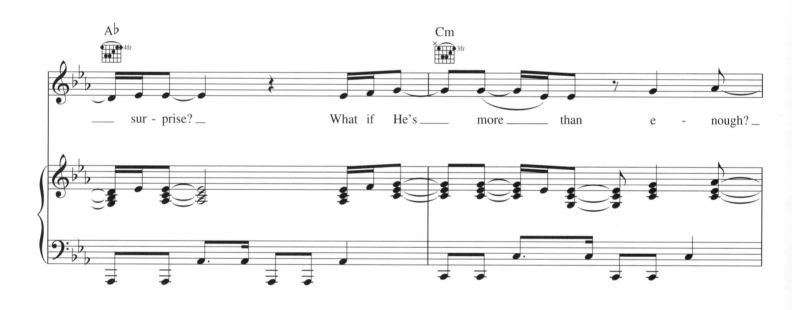

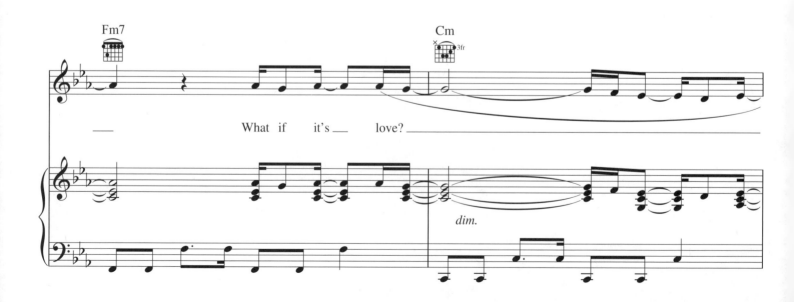

What if ___ it's ___

love? ___

# FOOL FOR YOU

Words and Music by
NICHOLE NORDEMAN

**Moderately bright**

There are times _ when faith and com-mon sense _ do not __ a - lign, _
I ad - mit __ that in my dark-est hours _ I've asked, _ "What if?" __

when hard - core ev - i - dence _ of You __ is hard _____ to _____ find. ____
What if __ we cre - a - ted _____ some kind ___ of man - made faith like this? _

# EVEN THEN

Words and Music by
NICHOLE NORDEMAN

# WHY?

Words and Music by
NICHOLE NORDEMAN

We rode in-to town

the oth - er day, _____ just me and my dad -
the sky _____ grew cloud - y and Dad - dy said I

# REAL TO ME

Words and Music by NICHOLE NORDEMAN,
JILL TOMALTY and JAY JOYCE

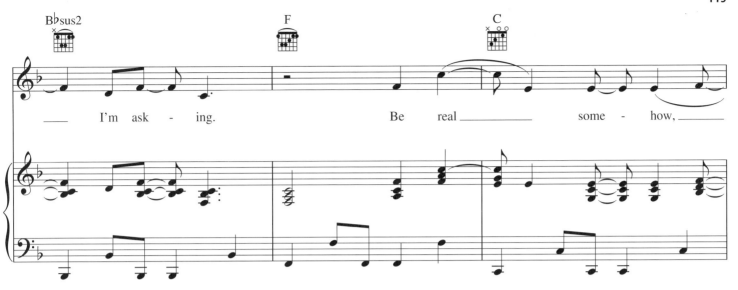

I'm ask - ing. Be real _____ some - how, _____

_____ more _____ than an - y - thing. _____ _____ than an - y - thing,

more _____ than an - y - thing. Be real _____

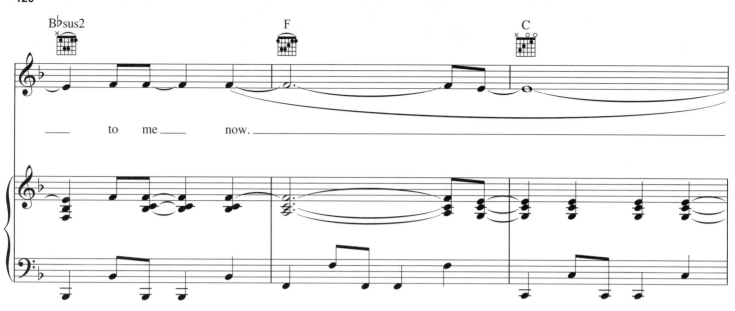

to me now.

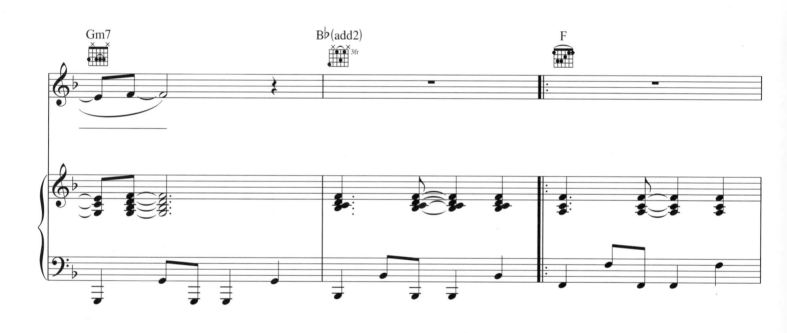

# WHO YOU ARE

Words and Music by NICHOLE NORDEMAN
and MARK HAMMOND

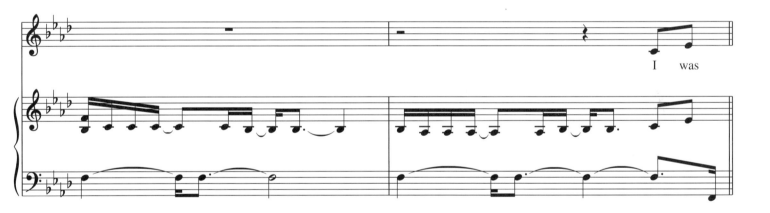

I was

cer - tain that __ I knew __ You at the ten - der age __ of twelve. You'd so

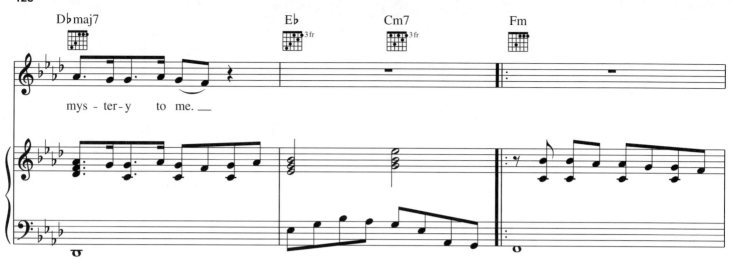

mys - ter-y    to  me. __

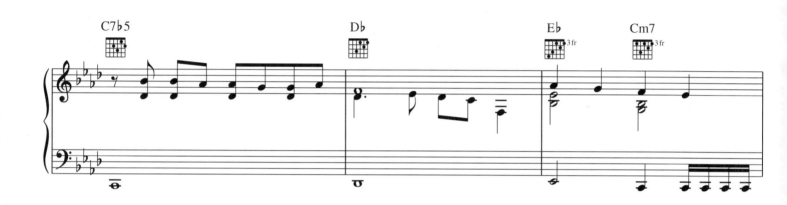

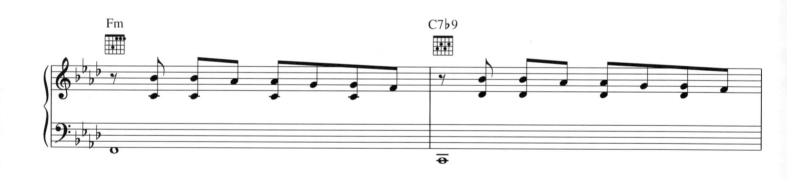

# RIVER GOD

Words and Music by
NICHOLE NORDEMAN

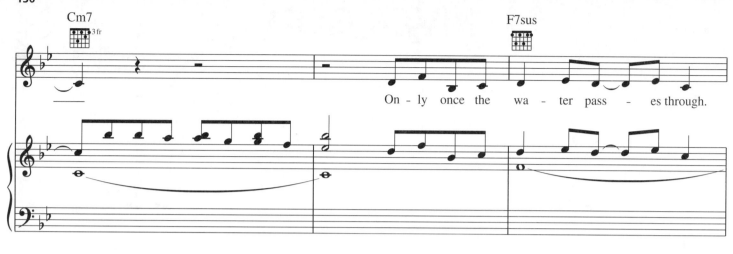

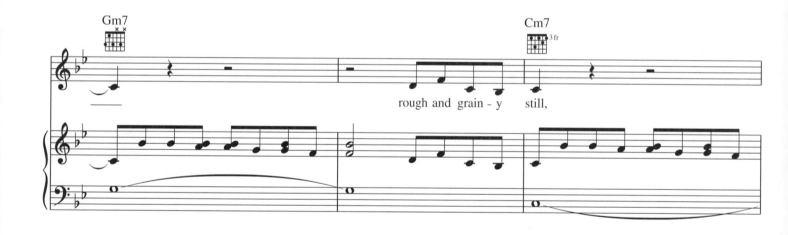

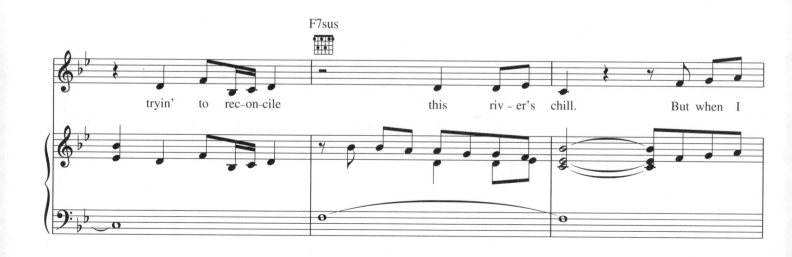

# More Contemporary Christian Folios from Hal Leonard

## Arranged for Piano, Voice and Guitar

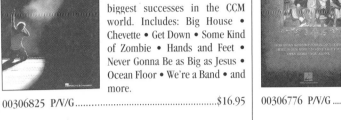

### AUDIO ADRENALINE – ADIOS: THE GREATEST HITS

17 of the best from one of the biggest successes in the CCM world. Includes: Big House • Chevette • Get Down • Some Kind of Zombie • Hands and Feet • Never Gonna Be as Big as Jesus • Ocean Floor • We're a Band • and more.

00306825 P/V/G........................$16.95

### THE VERY BEST OF AVALON – TESTIFY TO LOVE

All 16 songs from the 2003 compilation by this acclaimed vocal quartet: Adonai • Can't Live a Day • Don't Save It All for Christmas Day • Everything to Me • Give It Up • Knockin' on Heaven's Door • New Day • Pray • Testify to Love • and more.

00306526 P/V/G........................$16.95

### JEREMY CAMP – BEYOND MEASURE

This CD showcases Camp's powerful voice, which earned him back-to-back Male Vocalist of the Year GMA Music Awards. Our songbook features all 12 tracks, including the hit single "What It Means" and: Beyond Measure • Everything • Give Me Jesus • Let It Fade • Tonight • more.

00306854 P/V/G........................$16.95

### CASTING CROWNS – LIFESONG

11 contemporary rock/worship songs from this popular band's 2005 album. Includes: And Now My Lifesong Sings • Does Anybody Hear Her • Father, Spirit, Jesus • In Me • Lifesong • Love Them like Jesus • Praise You in This Storm • Prodigal • Set Me Free • Stained Glass Masquerade • While You Were Sleeping.

00306748 P/V/G........................$16.95

### THE BEST OF STEVEN CURTIS CHAPMAN

21 songs from this award-winning Contemporary Christian/Gospel legend, including: Dive • The Great Adventure • Heaven in the Real World • Live Out Loud • Magnificent Obsession • More to This Life • No Better Place • Remembering You • and more.

00306811 P/V/G........................$17.95

### DAVID CROWDER BAND COLLECTION

David Crowder's innovative alt-pop style has made him one of today's most popular worship leaders. This collection includes 16 of his best songs: Here Is Our King • No One like You • Open Skies • Our Love Is Loud • You Alone • and more.

00306776 P/V/G........................$16.95

### STEVE GREEN – THE ULTIMATE COLLECTION

25 songs from the hits collection for this gospel star who got his start backing up Sandi Patti and the Gaither Vocal Band in the mid-'70s. Includes: Find Us Faithful • He Is Good • People Need the Lord • We Believe • What Wondrous Love Is This • and more.

00306784 P/V/G........................$19.95

### KUTLESS – STRONG TOWER

The 2005 release by this Christian hard rock band hailing from Oregon includes 13 tracks: We Fall Down • Take Me In • Ready for You • Draw Me Close • Better Is One Day • I Lift My Eyes Up • Word of God Speak • Arms of Love • and more.

00306726 P/V/G........................$16.95

### BRIAN LITTRELL – WELCOME HOME

Matching folio to the former Backstreet Boy's solo Contemporary Christian release. Includes all 10 tracks: Angels and Heroes • I'm Alive • My Answer Is You • We Lift You Up • Welcome Home (You) • and more.

00306830 P/V/G........................$16.95

*Music Inspired by*
### THE CHRONICLES OF NARNIA

THE LION, THE WITCH AND THE WARDROBE
11 songs from the album featuring CCM artists. Includes: I Will Believe (Nichole Nordeman) • Lion (Rebecca St. James) • Remembering You (Steven Curtis Chapman) • Waiting for the World to Fall (Jars of Clay) • and more.

00313311 P/V/G........................$16.95

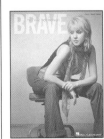

### NICHOLE NORDEMAN – BRAVE

11 tracks from the 2005 album by this talented singer-songwriter: Brave • Crimson • Gotta Serve Somebody • Hold On • Lay It Down • Live • No More Chains • Real to Me • Someday • We Build • What If.

00306729 P/V/G........................$16.95

### PHILLIPS, CRAIG & DEAN – THE ULTIMATE COLLECTION

31 of the greatest hits by this popular CCM trio. Includes: Crucified with Christ • Favorite Song of All • Here I Am to Worship • Lord, Let Your Glory Fall • Midnight Oil • Only You • Restoration • Shine on Us • This Is the Life • The Wonderful Cross • and more.

00306789 P/V/G........................$19.95

### MICHAEL W. SMITH – GREATEST HITS

2ND EDITION
25 of the best songs from this popular Contemporary Christian singer/songwriter, includes: Friends • I Will Be Here for You • Place in This World • Secret Ambition • This Is Your Time • You Are Holy (Prince of Peace) • and more.

00358186 P/V/G........................$17.95

### STARFIELD – BEAUTY IN THE BROKEN

Starfield wrote songs perfect for use in a modern church. Our matching folio to their 2006 release features all 11 tracks: Captivate • Everything Is Beautiful • Great Is the Lord • My Generation • Obsession • Unashamed • and more.

00306832 P/V/G........................$17.95

### SWITCHFOOT – NOTHING IS SOUND

Switchfoot's rock style and street-smart faith has given them widespread success in CCM and secular arenas. This songbook from their 2005 release features 12 songs: Daisy • Happy Is a Yuppie Word • Lonely Nation • The Setting Sun • Stars • more.

00306756 P/V/G........................$16.95

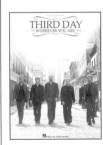

### THIRD DAY – WHEREVER YOU ARE

This popular rock band's 2005 release features "Cry Out to Jesus" plus: Carry My Cross • Communion • Eagles • How Do You Know • I Can Feel It • Keep on Shinin' • Love Heals Your Heart • Mountain of God • Rise Up • The Sun Is Shining • Tunnel.

00306766 P/V/G........................$16.95

### CHRIS TOMLIN – ARRIVING

Our matching folio to the 2004 release from this award-winning singer/songwriter and worship leader from Texas features all 11 songs, including the hit singles: Holy Is the Lord • How Great Is Our God • and Indescribable.

00306857 P/V/G........................$16.95

Prices, contents, and availability subject to change without notice.

0407